When Captain Arthur Phillip sailed into Botany Bay, on the east coast of Australia, in January 1788, he was unimpressed. The bay was unprotected and shallow and surrounded by poor soil and its shore was observed to be unproductive with scarce fresh water. Having led a fleet of ships halfway around the world to found a penal colony for British convicts, he decided to explore further north for a better location.

He found it just 12 kilometres up the coast. Port Jackson was an inlet discovered and named by Captain James Cook in 1770 although it was not extensively explored at the time. What Phillip found as he ventured up the inlet was, in his opinion, 'the finest harbour in the world'.

Named after the British Home Secretary Thomas Townshend (Lord Sydney), Sydney Cove was a well sheltered deep water anchorage with ample fresh water supplies. It was a perfect site for the first official British settlement on the Australian continent.

FOR THE FIRST TWO DECADES OF SYDNEY'S EXISTENCE THE COLONY WAS SO LACKING IN APPROPRIATE SKILLS AND TOOLS THAT THE MAJORITY OF BUILDINGS CONSTRUCTED WERE OF POOR QUALITY AND IN NEED OF CONSTANT MAINTENANCE.

The situation changed dramatically with the appointment of Major-General Lachlan Macquarie as Governor of New South Wales in 1810. Finding many structures throughout the settlement in a 'most ruinous state of decay', Macquarie implemented a set of building codes that dictated a minimum standard for any future construction. Teaming up with convicted forger and architect Francis Greenway, the Governor also commissioned a series of classically inspired public buildings including Hyde Park Barracks (1819) and St James Church (1824), both of which still stand today.

From the mid to late 19th century architectural trends in Sydney closely followed those adopted throughout the British Empire. Grand classical revival styles were used extensively for public and administrative buildings whilst well to do residents displayed their wealth with elaborate Victorian Italianate or sober Georgian home designs.

INTRODUCTION

The Rocks area of Sydney, named in reference to the local sandstone deposits from which many early buildings were constructed, is an architecturally unique enclave.

Located near the CBD of Australia's largest city, The Rocks has managed to avoid widespread re-development over the past 50 years and, as a result, possesses many well preserved commercial and residential structures dating from the 19th and early 20th centuries.

Located on the southern shore of Sydney Harbour the area now known as The Rocks had been inhabited by native Gadigal people of the Eora nation for centuries before European settlement. Shortly after the British colony of Sydney was established in 1788 numerous dwellings began to appear, although the majority were poorly built timber or brick structures.

The local abundant sandstone provided the material for many new buildings throughout the following decades, from the oldest residential structure, Cadmans Cottage (1816), to the former Maritime Services Board building (1952), currently the Museum of Contemporary Art.

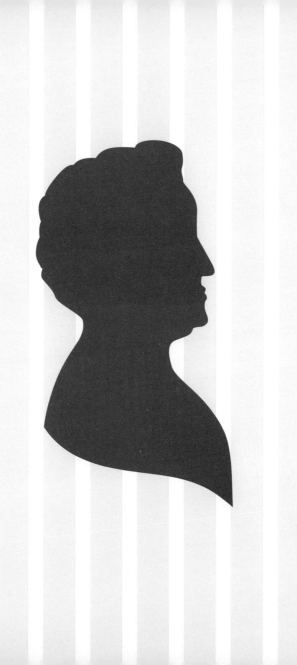

For much of its existence The Rocks area, being typical of many port settlements, was notorious for the various nefarious activities that patrons of its numerous taverns and brothels engaged in, particularly along the waterfront. By the end of the 19th century many residents were living in slum conditions. After an outbreak of bubonic plaque in 1900 the NSW Government took control of the area, and proceeded to demolish hundreds of dwellings ostensibly to pave the way for better housing conditions.

The building of Sydney Harbour Bridge (1923) and the Cahill Expressway (1955-57) resulted in the loss of many more buildings and it was not until the 1970s that widespread concern was raised about the disappearance of much of The Rocks early built heritage.

Passionate community based activism and trade union supported 'green bans' (a form of strike action for environmental or conservation purposes) eventually resulted in widespread protection and heritage listing of many significant Rocks buildings.

Today The Rocks, through its architecture, provides a rich and varied glimpse into the development of the city of Sydney, from settlement through to the first half of the 20th century.

MSB BUILDING

Previously known as the Sydney Harbour Trust, by 1936 the organisation responsible for all NSW commercial and recreational marine activities had been renamed the Maritime Services Board and was in the process of relocating its offices. The site chosen had been occupied by the Commissariat Stores, built by convict labour, from 1809. By 1939 the buildings had been demolished and plans drawn up in preparation for the construction of the new MSB premises. World War Two intervened, however, and it was not until 1949 that the foundation stone was laid.

By the time it was completed in 1952 the new building's heavy stripped classical exterior and art deco interiors were considered old fashioned, especially compared to the emerging post-war Modernist styles. It is nonetheless a fine example of inter-war styled administrative architecture, built around a steel and concrete frame with yellow Maroubra sandstone-faced walls. The severe symmetry of the 'H' plan office is emphasised by the central tower with its expressed vertical elements and polished granite framed entrance. External decoration is limited to a bas-relief above the entrance doors and sandstone carvings of a ship's propeller, wheel and anchor below the tower clock. Internally there is extensive use of polished Wombeyan and green marble in addition to much decorative maritime-themed metalwork.

The MSB moved to a CBD location in 1989 and the Circular Quay building has, since 1991, been home to the Museum of Contemporary Art.

GRAYSON
PERRY
MY PRETTY
LITTLE ART
CAREER

In 1798 convict John Cadman arrived in Sydney having been found guilty of stealing a horse in Bewdley, Worcestershire. Working as a coxswain on a government boat from 1809 he was given a free pardon by Governor Macquarie in 1821 and went on to be master of the Cutter 'Mars' four years later. In 1827 he was promoted to the post of Superintendent of Government Boats and moved into the rough stone cottage on The Rocks shoreline with his family.

The cottage had been home to three previous Government coxswains but is now known by the name of its last and longest serving resident, the position being abolished after Cadman's retirement in 1845. Constructed in 1816 of sandstone in a simple Colonial Georgian style, the cottage has been used over the years as headquarters of the Sydney Water Police (1845-64) and the Sydney Sailors Home (1865-1970).

Restoration began in 1972 shortly after heritage listing (as Sydney's oldest residential structure) and the cottage is now open to the public, serving as the Sydney Harbour National Park Information Centre.

THE ORIENT HOTEL

The site on which the Orient Hotel is located was once part of Sydney's first hospital complex, founded shortly after the First Fleet landed in 1788. The land was subdivided in 1841 and lots 1 and 2 were purchased by butcher James Chapman who, in 1842, proceeded to construct a three-storey, ten-room residence and an adjoining single-storey shop. By the time of Chapman's death in 1856 the residence had been converted to a licensed premises named the Marine Hotel. Witnessing a succession of owners and publicans, as well as name changes, over the years, the hotel has been known as the Orient since 1885 when it was purchased by Walter McCombie. The name was possibly inspired by the fact that from 1877 ships of the Orient Steam Navigation Line berthed at the nearby, newly developed Campbell's Wharf.

By the 1930s the original single-storey shop and subsequent shed structures had been demolished to make way for extensions to both the Argyle and George Street facades. These additions closely matched the building's Colonial Georgian style with its plain walls, rectangular windows and curved corner facade.

One of Sydney's oldest continuously licensed hotels, the Orient exemplifies the significant historical nature of The Rock's built environment.

THE ROCKS
POLICE STATION

As official Colonial Architect for NSW (1862-90) James Barnet designed numerous classically inspired public buildings including the General Post Office (1891) and the Department of Lands building (1893). His smaller projects included 155 police stations located throughout the state, of which The Rocks building is surely the most elaborate. The two-storey facade, comprising a central arched entrance flanked by single window bays, resembles a Palladian-inspired water gate (a structure allowing easy, dry access from a quay or harbour to a castle or town wall). Many elements, including the piers, quoins and voussoirs, are heavily articulated, lending a highly textured quality to the surface.

Within the pediment above the arch are the initials VR (Victoria Regina), referring to Queen Victoria, whilst the arch's keystone displays a carved lion's head (representing British justice) holding a policeman's truncheon in its mouth. Currently made of hardwood the original truncheon was possibly bronze but, as a result of previous thefts, has been replaced on numerous occasions.

The building operated as No. 4 Police Station until 1974, briefly serving as a U.S. Navy lock up during the Second World War. Currently occupied by a café, the structure is a distinctive and intact example of a 19th century Victorian metropolitan police station, retaining many of the architectural details that identify its specific role.

✪ OF NOTE

Hospital plaque (former Rocks police station)

Located below the left ground level window bay of the police station is a plaque commemorating the site of Sydney's first hospital. Established as a series of tents soon after the First Fleet arrived in 1788, it soon developed into a more substantial complex of timber and brick structures boasting a well-equipped laboratory and dispensary. Further enhanced by a prefabricated portable hospital that arrived with the Second Fleet in 1790, the facility eventually covered an area bounded by Globe, George, Harrington and Argyle Streets. It was replaced in 1816 by a new hospital (Sydney Hospital, which remains in operation) on Macquarie Street.

✪ OF NOTE

Suez Canal (1840s)

Running between George and Harrington Streets, the Suez Canal (thought to be a pun on the word 'sewers') is a rare original 19th century laneway with a notorious reputation. Brothels, opium dens and sly grog shops once satisfied the vices of those who dared to venture into the seedy thoroughfare.

It was also a known haunt of the violent 'Rocks Push' street gang whose female associates would lure unsuspecting drunks into the lane where they would be persuaded by fist and boot to surrender their valuables.

BRITISH SEAMEN'S HOTEL

When graziers John and William Gill opened their newly-built licenced premises in 1886 they retained the name of the hotel that had previously existed on the site. In fact, a public house of some kind had operated there since 1830 when Caleb Slater became innkeeper of what was then known as the 'Kings Head'.

The British Seamen's Hotel is an early example of what is now referred to as Federation Queen Anne, an Australian take on a style that became popular in the U.K from the late 19th century. Emerging as part of the Arts and Crafts movement this revival style utilised picturesque motifs and materials inspired by romantic notions of pre-industrial architecture. In this case the style is expressed in the building's alternating facade treatment of rendered banding and brickwork, scrolled pediments and arched, multi-casement windows. Additional decorative flourishes include bands of floral themed motifs below the second-storey arch windows and dentil courses under the cornices, both of which became frequently applied features of Australian hotel architecture after Federation (1901).

From 1899 the pub was known as the Hughes's Family Hotel, before becoming McCarthy's Hotel in the 1920s. Around 1928 the building became a boarding house, then offices until major conservation work was undertaken in 1995 resulting in a highly original exterior and interior.

SUSANNAH PLACE
MUSEUM

Continuously occupied for almost 150 years, the four terrace houses that make up Susannah Place offer a rare insight into domestic working class life in The Rocks throughout the 19th and 20th centuries. They were built by Edward Riley who, along with his wife Mary and their niece Susannah (after whom the terraces were named), lived in number 62 for nearly 30 years whilst leasing out numbers 58, 60 and 64 to a variety of tenants. Riley and his family arrived in Sydney in 1838 as assisted immigrants, somehow finding the means to purchase the land on Gloucester Street just four years later, in the midst of a depression, for the substantial sum of 450 pounds.

The terraces are constructed of colonial bond brickwork (where the bricks are laid in alternating rows of stretcher and header configuration) on a sandstone foundation. Simply detailed and proportioned, each three-level terrace originally comprised six rooms with a basement kitchen and outhouses. The original shingle roof, surrounded by a sandstone-capped parapet, was replaced with corrugated iron in the late 19th century.

The last tenants,
Ellen and Dennis Marshall,
moved out of number 62 in 1990.
In 1992, after extensive restoration work,
the terraces were put in the hands of the
Historic Houses Trust of NSW and opened
as a museum. Visitors enter through
number 64, the corner terrace
which operated as a shop
until 1935.

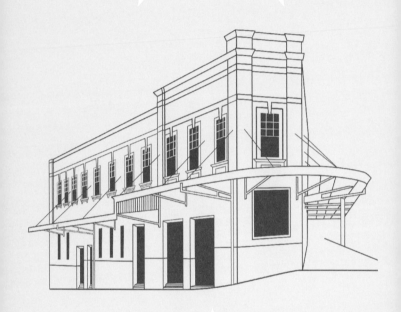

THE AUSTRALIAN HOTEL

Sited prominently on a street corner, the Australian Hotel replaced a pub of the same name that had been demolished due to the realignment of Cumberland Street around 1907. Designed in an Italianate style the two-storey structure is rendered brick (partially exposed at the first level) punctuated by tall rectangular windows and topped by a stepped parapet.

Subtle moulded banding decorates the upper facade which was repainted in original 1920s colours during extensive conservation works in 1991-92. The interior, with its unique split level bar, is relatively intact with many original fittings and decorative features.

The original construction plans included two adjoining shops, one on Cumberland Street, used as a grocery store, and the other on Gloucester Street. Both spaces now operate as part of the hotel; the former grocery store is used as a kitchen and restaurant whilst the Gloucester Street site is now a wine shop.

THE ARGYLE CUT

As the settlement of Sydney grew throughout the early 19th century increasing demands were made to improve access between The Rocks and Millers Point. The natural sandstone barrier dividing the two areas was a serious impediment to both the transport and mercantile activities that were increasing at an enormous pace, especially after the development of Darling Harbour. Vehicles travelling between Sydney Cove and Darling Harbour had to negotiate a convoluted route whilst pedestrians braved a crudely made and rapidly deteriorating set of stairs cut into the rock.

Wealthy landowner and merchant Alexander Berry put forward a proposal for a cutting, intending to profit from the project by creating it as a toll road. Governor Richard Bourke, however, decided that the project should be undertaken by the government and, in 1832, Governor Bourke instructed architect Edward Hallen to prepare plans. Work began in 1843, undertaken by convict labour under the harsh supervision of Tim Lane who motivated the workers with inspirational statements such as 'by the help of God and the strong arm of the flogger, you'll get fifty before breakfast tomorrow!' It was soon apparent, however, that the task was beyond simple hand tools and the cut was finally completed in 1859 by Sydney Municipal Council with the aid of explosives and better skilled council workers.

Around 1912 the Argyle Stairs (Arched entrance, on the right when facing west up Argyle Street) were constructed to link Argyle Street with Gloucester (Gloucester Walk) and Cumberland Streets.

SYDNEY OBSERVATORY

Located on what is appropriately known as Observatory Hill, the present structure was the third such facility to be established in the colony. The first was set up on Dawes Point soon after the arrival of the First Fleet in order to observe a comet that was calculated to appear in 1790. A second observatory was built in Parramatta in 1821 by Governor Sir Thomas Brisbane but it was closed in 1847 due to neglect of the facilities by its superintendent.

Plans were drawn up for a third observatory in 1850 but it wasn't until 1857 that construction commenced. Completed in 1859, the two-storey sandstone structure is Italianate in style with a campanile-like tower. Floors are externally expressed with string courses and the corners feature articulated quoins which, along with the window surrounds and eaves, display fine stone workmanship. In 1874 the original south telescope dome was replaced with a larger copper clad structure to accommodate a newly acquired German Schroeder telescope which can still be seen today. The second dome, along with the west wing, was added in 1876. Initially the prime purpose of the new building was to be time keeping using a time ball mechanism. This can be seen atop the tower and is still in use, though for historical rather than practical reasons. Every day at 1:00pm the ball is dropped and then raised again via an electric motor, as opposed to manually as was the case originally.

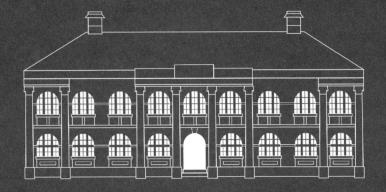

✪ OF NOTE

Agar Steps (c1870)

Named after Thomas Agar, a well-known resident of
The Rocks area, the Agar Steps were constructed to form
a link between Observatory Hill and Kent Street. Comprised
of 108 steps they overlook the former Kent Street Quarry
and are considered the best surviving example of stairways
providing access from the hill to the lower Rocks precinct.

OLD FORT STREET SCHOOL

The New South Wales Marine Corps was a volunteer unit created to guard convicts on the ships of the First Fleet. In 1792 it was replaced by the New South Wales Corps, an infamous regiment which later earned the nickname the "Rum Corps" due to its liquor trading monopoly. Initially housed in tents, the regiment constructed its proper military barracks in Wynyard and, in 1815, Governor Macquarie commissioned a military hospital to provide medical services for the soldiers.

The barracks moved in 1848 to Paddington and the hospital was converted for use as a government run, non-denominational school, the first such institution in the country. Initially called the Model School it was later known as Fort Street High School.

Constructed in rendered brick the building is Colonial Georgian in style overlaid with Classical Revival features. The two-storey symmetrical facade is decorated with three separate entablature forms supported by eight pilasters, each of which is topped by a Corinthian capital. The Royal coat of arms of the United Kingdom sits above the central entablature. The arched windows were originally unglazed forming open loggias on both levels.

Co-educational from the beginning, due to increasing student numbers the male students moved to new premises in Petersham in 1916 whilst the girls remained at Fort Street until 1975. The building now operates as the NSW headquarters of the National Trust.

Following the Agar Steps down will place you on Kent Street, one of the longest streets in Sydney. Running north-south between Walsh Bay and Darling Harbour, it was named in 1810 by Governor Macquarie in honour of the Duke of Kent, the younger brother of King George III.

The eastern side of the street, between the Agar Steps and Argyle Street, was once known as the Kent Street Quarry. Operating from the 1830s to the early 1860s it provided sandstone for many of the notable buildings from the era that survive today, including the Sydney Observatory and Garrison Church. Part of the quarry can be seen behind the tennis courts beside the Agar Steps.

The north end of Kent Street is lined with a rich variety of 19th century terrace houses. Located at numbers 37-47, Alfreds Terrace is a notable original example of domestic Georgian style architecture. Built in 1865 the exposed sandstone facade features simple decorative elements such as 12 pane windows, stone cornices above the doorways and a projecting roof parapet.

On the corner of Kent and Argyle Streets is the former Millers Point Post Office. Constructed in 1891, it is a unique example of the Federation Free Classical style with some interesting stylistic details. The brickwork is formed using a mix of Flemish bond and stretcher bond methods. Multi-panel sash windows flank the first storey arched entrance and an oculus form on the second, while the roof is decorated with a convoluted parapet with a rendered coping.

LORD NELSON HOTEL

Reputed to be Sydney's oldest continuously licenced pub, the Lord Nelson Hotel began trading in 1842, the same year in which the city was officially incorporated. The building was constructed around 1836 by William Wells who initially used it as his residence. Wells occupied the hotel on and off until 1870 when the premises was taken over by John Henwood and Alfred C Wells, possibly a relative. Although various changes have been made to the interiors over the years, during the 1990s the exterior was restored in a manner that reflects the original appearance of the building.

Built of sandstone quarried from nearby Observatory Hill the hotel represents the Old Colonial Regency style that was popular in Australia during the early 19th century. Rectangular sash windows punctuate the facades with large, fixed, timber framed glazing on either side of the corner entrance. The Argyle Street and corner entrance are both arched with decorative fanlights. Unusually, for a large building in this style, rendering of the stonework is restricted to a painted ground level band running along the Argyle Street facade and continuing down the sloping Kent Street side, articulated by a broad string course.

The interior decor, with its exposed timber roof beams and floorboards, has an appropriately nautical feel and includes an original copy of the Times newspaper of 7th November, 1805 with details of the Battle of Trafalgar and Lord Nelson's death.

WALSH BAY
WHARVES

Built as part of the early 20th century reconstruction of the Millers Point area, the Walsh Bay Wharves were a vital component of Sydney's maritime infrastructure until the 1970s. The complex is comprised of a long shore wharf (Pier 1), four finger wharves (Piers 2-9) and a series of shore sheds along Hickson Road.

The wharves are constructed of timber piles of up to 40 metres driven into the bedrock below. Timber planks originally formed the decking, later being replaced with concrete. The wharf sheds are simply built using the post and beam method with steel trusses and the walls and roofs are clad mainly in galvanised iron. The shore sheds are constructed in a similar manner with the addition of brick facades facing Hickson Road. The two-storey facades of the three separate structures reflect the popular Federation Free Style of the time with multiple decorative banding, expressed brick pilasters and geometric parapet forms. The shed facade fronting piers eight and nine is particularly ornate with two large arched windows framed by pointed stone voussoirs. Various industrial artefacts can be seen throughout the complex including hoists, floor hatches, hydraulic pumps and wool bale elevators.

From 1982, after years of disuse, the wharves were gradually redeveloped into an entertainment and cultural precinct and are now home to restaurants, apartments and the Sydney Theatre Company.

HERO OF
WATERLOO HOTEL

Sharing both a corner location and reference in its name to
a British military legend, the Hero of Waterloo can also claim,
along with the Lord Nelson Hotel, to be one of Sydney's oldest
drinking establishments. The building was constructed in 1844
by Scottish stonemason George Paton, who also worked on the
Garrison Church. A year later the pub was licenced and was
soon busy serving a clientele of seafarers and colonial troops.

The three-storey structure is built from rough faced sandstone
with a broad rendered string course running between the first
and second levels. Georgian style rectangular sash windows
punctuate the facade and the hipped roof is decorated with
simple parapets. The interior has witnessed few dramatic changes
over the years apart from the expansion of the main bar in 1928
when a partition wall was removed.

⭐ OF NOTE

Parbury Ruins (Corner Windmill & Pottinger Streets)

The remains of an early 19th century stone cottage can be seen at
this site. Discovered during excavation work for a new apartment
complex in 2000, and subsequently preserved in the basement
level, the dwelling was built by Hugh Noble sometime around 1820.
It was sold to Thomas Street in 1831 who added a basement and
kitchen in 1835. By the 1860s the cottage had been abandoned
and partly demolished. Please note that although access is
by appointment only, the site can be illuminated and
viewed through the glass.

The pub's cellar, which can be visited, features a secret tunnel that leads to the harbour. Legend has it that during the 19th century it was used for various nefarious activities including rum smuggling and the shanghaiing of drunken patrons to crew undermanned ships. True or not these stories add to the historical texture of this long standing establishment.

THE GARRISON
CHURCH

By the late 1830s increasing maritime activities around Millers Point were drawing a larger number of Anglican parishioners to the area than the sole church (St Philip's, established 1797) could cope with. A community meeting was convened in December 1839 resulting in a petition being sent to Governor Sir George Gipps for the establishment of a new parish. Permission was granted in January 1840 and the foundation stone for the new church was laid on the 23rd of June by Bishop William Broughton. Although construction began rapidly the depression of the 1840s soon slowed things down and by 1844 Bishop Broughton decided to allow Rev. John Couch Grylls to commence services in the partially built church. In 1855 architect Edmund Blacket was commissioned to complete the building and by 1878 the church appeared as it does to this day.

Gothic in style, the church is constructed of locally quarried sandstone with a slate roof. Externally the wide central nave is flanked on the north and south elevations by buttress forms and stone tracery windows, five to each side. The windows are decorated with label moulds and foliage bosses whilst the corner buttresses are topped by elaborate carved stone pinnacles. Internally two stone arcades, formed by five arches, run the length of the nave.

During its early years the church was regularly attended by garrison troops stationed at the nearby Dawes Point Battery, an association with the military that continued well into the 20th century.

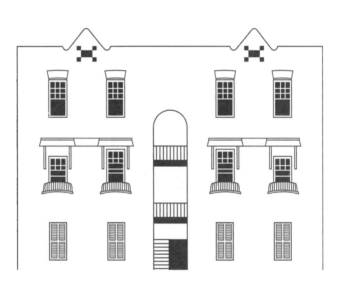

WORKERS FLATS

In 1900, on the pretext of eradicating the recent outbreak of bubonic plague from the area, the NSW Government took control of and demolished hundreds of dwellings it considered slums. Over the next few years a process of reconstruction was initiated and a new supply of worker housing was built throughout Millers Point and The Rocks.

Walter Liberty Vernon migrated to Australia from England in 1883 and by 1890 was appointed government architect, working in the NSW Department of Public Works. Tasked with designing workers flats on Lower Fort Street, he drew up a plan for five semi-detached blocks of three storeys each.

Since arriving in Sydney, Vernon had become well known for his fondness for the prevailing Federation architectural styles, and the new flats gave him the opportunity to express this affinity. Designed in what is now referred to as the Federation Free Style, each block is constructed in red brick with darker decorative elements around the sash windows. A brick string course delineates the ground and first floors and alternating triangular and arched gable parapets crown each block. Curiously, block 40-42 has its upper facade rendered with more decorative features including expressed brickwork arches above the second floor windows and entablatures with dentils above those on the third floor. An interesting design feature between each block is the use of projecting, angled window bays for the upper floors, enabling maximum light to enter the rooms.

Retiring from his government post in 1911, Walter Vernon died in 1914, leaving behind a rich legacy of Federation inspired architecture throughout Sydney and New South Wales.

In 1825 Robert Crawford, Principal Clerk to the Colonial Secretary, wrote to his father in Scotland informing him that "I am just finishing a house near Dawes Battery – I call it Clyde Bank, it looks into Cockle Bay and is ten minutes' walk from the office." Crawford had arrived in Sydney in 1821 and was granted the land on which he built his residence in 1823.

The two-storey rendered brick house is a highly original domestic example of Old Colonial Regency architecture. Windows and doors are symmetrically arranged with four French doors on the first level (exhibiting offset glazing beads typical of the Regency style) and five bays of sash windows on the second. The central window is an unusual feature being divided into two narrow panels by a stone pier. The slate verandah roof is supported by ten Doric columns and elegantly matches the hipped villa roof above. Both the garage and structure linking it to the main building are relatively recent additions designed in appropriate period styles.

Unfortunately Robert Crawford wasn't able to enjoy his new home for long, being forced to sell it in 1828 due to financial difficulties.

✪ OF NOTE

Iron Urinal

Originally located on Observatory
Hill, the cast iron 'pissoir' on George Street
(under the Sydney Harbour Bridge) was fabricated
around 1880 as part the council's program to provide
public toilets throughout the city. Featuring highly
ornate panels decorated in the Italianate style,
the facility was designed by an English firm founded
by George Jennings, a sanitary engineer who
invented the first public flush toilets.

THE MERCANTILE HOTEL

Trading continuously since 1915, the Mercantile Hotel was built as part of brewer Tooth & Co.'s expansion throughout the early 20th century. In 1835 John Tooth started a brewery in Sydney with his brother-in-law John Newnham. Business was good and by the late 19th century the Tooth family had interests in a variety of fields including real estate and banking. The dawn of the 20th century saw Tooth & Co as the dominant brewer in NSW and the company continued to expand via the acquisition of rival breweries and malt producers. Building or buying hotels was another effective way of cornering the beer market due to the tied house system, meaning the licensee was obligated to market the brewer's products exclusively. This practice was outlawed in 1974.

Constructed on the site previously occupied by the Mercantile Rowing Club Hotel (1878) the building is considered a subdued example of the Federation Free Style. The red brick facade, punctuated by single pane rectangular sash windows, is decorated with rendered cream bands. A simple corniche form sits below the roof, which features ornate iron balustrades. The most ostentatious feature of the exterior is the glazed green tiled section of wall at street level which, stylistically, is more closely associated with Art Nouveau than Federation architecture.

One of Australia's oldest companies, Tooth & Co. witnessed many changes of fortune over subsequent decades, ceasing to function as an independent entity in 1983 after the first of many corporate takeovers by various business concerns.

AUSTRALASIAN STEAM
NAVIGATION COMPANY

The Hunter River Steam Navigation Company was founded in 1839, reforming in 1851 as the Australasian Steam Navigation Company. Acquiring prominent waterfront land in 1876 the company proceeded to construct the new premises that would serve as its main offices and warehouse.

The building was designed by William Wardell, an architect who had moved to Sydney in 1878 having primarily worked in Melbourne since his arrival from England in 1858. His previous works included Victoria's Government House (1876) and St Mary's Cathedral in Sydney, one of the largest ecclesiastical buildings in Australia. With the ASN project Wardell introduced a very early example of Federation Anglo-Dutch architecture to the city. The first floor stone base gives way to red-brown brick work with red brick decorative features in the form of window head arches and horizontal banding.

The warehouse facades each have a central loading bay topped by a brickwork arch. Rising five floors they are crowned by stone capped Dutch gables featuring an oculus, below which can be seen the old hoist pulleys. The facades facing Hickson Road are staggered and appear to descend below the rising street. The large fortress-like structure sitting atop the warehouses is a water tower that was added in 1894. The adjoining office is designed in a similar manner to the warehouse facades with the addition of a prominent central clock tower.

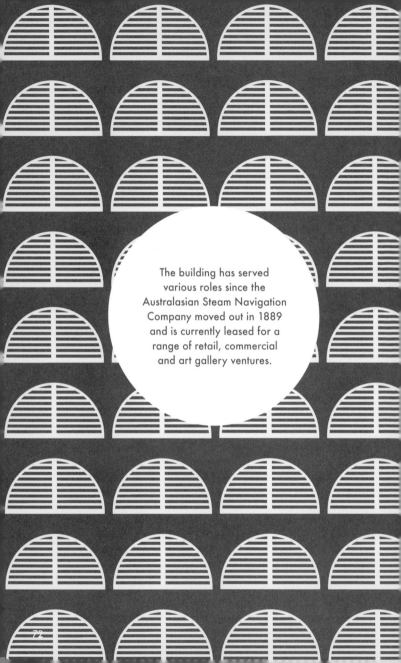

The building has served various roles since the Australasian Steam Navigation Company moved out in 1889 and is currently leased for a range of retail, commercial and art gallery ventures.

✪ OF NOTE

Campbell's Stores / 1851-61 / 7-27 Circular Quay West

Comprised of 11 bays of three storeys each,
Campbell's Stores are a rare surviving example of
mid-19th century Georgian warehouse architecture on
Sydney's foreshore. Robert Campbell was a Scottish merchant
who arrived in Australia in 1798, and built up a thriving
business over the following decades. Initially two storeys high,
a third brick level was added to each bay around 1882.

OBSERVER
HOTEL

Commissioned by brewer Tooth & Co., the Observer Hotel is
another example of a Federation Free Style design incorporating
Art Nouveau elements. Built on what was originally part of the old
hospital's medicinal plant gardens (1788-1816), the hotel replaced
an earlier licenced premises called the Observer Tavern (1848).
An uncommon name for a public house, it is thought to have been
inspired by the construction of the Sydney Observatory in the
same year.

The three-storey facade is red brick highlighted with mustard yellow
cement rendering. Central recessed balconies on the second and
third storeys are flanked on either side by two bays of sash windows.
An unbroken cornice with dentil moulding crowns the top floor and
marks the transition of the expressed bays into parapet elements.
The moulded floral motifs within each element, along with the
Observer Hotel script on the pediment, reflect the emerging
Art Nouveau decorative style that was increasingly being used
in early 20th century Australian hotel architecture.

Although the interior has been altered significantly over the years, the hotel's exterior remains original and is a significant surviving example of The Rocks post-plague rebuilding effort.

FRANCIS GREENWAY

(1777-1837)

Partly responsible for Sydney's earliest surviving residential structure (supervising the design and construction of Cadmans Cottage in 1816), Francis Howard Greenway came to Australia as a convict in February 1814.

He was born in Gloucestershire, near Bristol, and went on to become an architect of some merit before bankruptcy led him to commit the crime of forgery. Sentenced to death, Greenway was lucky to have his sentence later commuted to 14 years transportation to the colony of New South Wales.

Arriving in Sydney with architectural portfolio and letters of recommendation in hand, Greenway was soon granted permission to seek private work to support himself and his family who had arrived in March 1814.

NSW Governor Lachlan Macquarie was keen to improve the quality of civic buildings in the colony and, impressed by Greenway's credentials, commissioned him to design a variety of structures from 1816 onwards.

Greenway's first project, the lighthouse at the entrance to Port Jackson, so impressed the Governor that he was emancipated and given the role of Acting Civil Architect. Over the next few years Greenway was responsible for the design of numerous prominent buildings including Hyde Park Barracks (1819), St James Church (1824) and Old Government House.

He also designed the obelisk that sits in Macquarie Park in central Sydney. Employed as a point from which to record distances to various locations in NSW, it shares the park with an anchor from the 'Sirius', a ship from the First Fleet.

Greenway fell out of favour with Macquarie over what the Governor took to be increasingly exorbitant fees and, in 1822, the architect was dismissed from his post by incoming Governor Thomas Brisbane. Although he continued in private practice Greenway never attained his previous success and remained bitter over his treatment to the end. He died of typhoid on his farm near Newcastle in 1837.

Many of his buildings have survived to the present day and are celebrated as significant and valued examples of Sydney's early built heritage. This led, rather ironically for a convicted forger, to his portrait being used on Australia's first ten dollar note.

THE ROCKS TIMELINE
1788-1826

Pre-1788 Occupied for thousands of years by indigenous tribes, the area now known as The Rocks was most recently home to the Gadigal or Eora people.

1788 The First Fleet arrives in Sydney Cove on January 26 under the command of Captain Arthur Phillip, the first Governor of NSW.

1793 The first free settlers arrive.

1808 Governor William Bligh is deposed by members of the NSW Corps. The event becomes known as the Rum Rebellion.

1810 Governor Lachlan Macquarie initiates extensive town planning and building reforms.

1816 Convict architect Francis Greenway supervises the construction of Cadmans Cottage. In the same year he also draws up plans for Sydney's first lighthouse, completed in 1818.

1823 Population of The Rocks area is estimated to be around 1200, the majority convicts and their children.

1826 One of the first substantial buildings is erected on Argyle Street. Constructed of stone, it serves as Sydney's first Customs House.

THE ROCKS TIMELINE
1840-1923

1840 The end of convict transportation to NSW.

1843 Construction of the Argyle Cut commences.

1850s Land subdivision and housing developments, along with paving and drainage works, begin to transform The Rocks and Millers Point into a more diversely populated neighbourhood.

1870 Last British troops depart the colony.

1888 Sydney celebrates its centenary.

1900 Bubonic plague breaks out in Millers Point, eventually resulting in the demolition of hundreds of dwellings throughout the area.

1901 Federation of the six colonies, establishing the nation of Australia.

1923 Construction of the Sydney Harbour Bridge begins, resulting in the realignment of streets and demolition of various structures in Millers Point and The Rocks.

GLOSSARY

Boss: A decorative protrusion of stone or wood

Buttress: A structure of masonry or brick used to provide lateral support to a wall

Campanile: Italian term for bell tower

Classical Order: A principal component of classical architecture comprising base, shaft, capital and entablature

Colonial Georgian/Regency: An Australian take on similar English styles emphasising symmetry and proportion. Georgian was generally sparsely decorated as opposed to the Regency style which incorporated subtle classical elements and motifs. Popular from settlement to the mid-19th century.

Coping: The capping or covering of a wall

Corinthian: One of the five classical orders, characterised by acanthus leaves decorating the capitals

Cornice: A continuous horizontal moulding crowning a building or aperture

Dentil Moulding: A small block used in repetition as a decorative feature on a cornice

Entablature: The structure above the capital comprising architrave, frieze and cornice

Facade: An exterior side of a building, often referring to the front

Federation Style: Encompassing various revival styles popular in England around 1890-1915 (including Queen Anne and Edwardian) Federation architecture utilised, amongst other elements, extensive brickwork and decorative roof features.

Freestone: A soft stone used in masonry for carving, moulding and tracery (eg sandstone)

Frieze: The central component of the entablature, often decorated with a relief design

Gable: The triangular part of a wall between the sloping faces of a pitched roof

Gallery: A platform raised above a church floor

Ionic: One of the five classical orders, characterised by a scroll-like ornament decorating the capital and often fluted shaft

Label Mould: A projecting element over an opening

Loggia: A covered exterior gallery enclosed on one side by arcades or colonnades.

Mansard: French style four-sided roof

Nave: The main body of a church building

Palladian: A style inspired by the 16th century architect Andrea Palladio. Primarily based on principles of symmetry, perspective and values of the formal classical temple architecture of Greece and Rome.

Parapet: A vertical extension of the facade wall at the edge of a roof

Pavilion: A structural emphasis placed at the end of a symmetrical building's wings

Pediment: A classical triangular shaped structure placed above the entablature of a building

Pier: An upright element or section providing structural support

Pilasters: A column feature projecting from the face of a wall (as opposed to a free standing column)

Portico: A porch extending from the main body of a building

Pulpit: The raised stand for speakers in a church

String Course: A thin horizontal band, usually of stone or brick, running along a wall to delineate floors

Quoin: Cornerstones of a wall, often rusticated.

Rustication: A masonry technique used to accentuate the joins between stone blocks. The face of each block is also often given a rough or patterned finish to further delineate each stone.

Voussoir: A wedge shaped element that forms part of an arch.

☞

THE WALK

....

The Footpath Guide to
The Rocks architecture in
Sydney takes approximately
1.5 hours to complete.